Broken:

For the Ones Picking Up the Pieces

Moonsoulchild

Broken: For the Ones Picking Up the Pieces

Welcome to my healing journey.

I will take you down a very personal, raw, and triggering path. Please, understand these are my experiences of feeling my lowest. These are the times I felt I was broken. In these pieces I share with you, I only hope they bring you the healing you're currently searching for. I only hope they bring you towards peace. I can't speak on what I haven't felt, lived, or currently going through. Everything you're about to read is straight from the deepest parts of my soul. Some may be dark. Some may be hard to read. Some may inspire you. This collection isn't to keep you in that dark place, it's to inspire you to leave that dark place behind. You may feel broken, but you never were. I'm going to tell you why.

Hold on, it's going to be a wild ride.

I'm not here to paint you the perfect picture of life. I'm here to give you the raw, uncut, emotional version. I'm here to show you how my life was once a disaster but turned into something beautiful.

You may feel lost now, not knowing who to trust or what direction to go next. You may feel like you have no more love to give, because you gave all you could to someone who destroyed you. You may feel true love won't ever make its way to you because the universe keeps throwing you lessons instead of blessings. You may feel under a lot of pressure to get to a place in life before you reach a certain age due to society expectations. You may feel like giving up because the more you give, the more pain you end up in. You may feel you're worthless because the people you invest your time in make you believe so. You may feel a lot of things at this moment, but you will overcome them all. This facade the world has you believing is your mind overthinking. Trust your heart. Trust your intuition. The universe has this way of taking you through hell just to find your worth. Trust it, you need to see how special you truly are.

"You're currently picking up the pieces, one at a time, while learning not everyone deserves to love you, or be loved by you."

Broken: For the Ones Picking Up the Pieces

Picking up the pieces may sting, being reminded of the memories of the reasons you loved them. The good moments will flood your mind, your heart will try and fight it off. I know they say to always remember the good, but when it's time to part ways you need to remember the reason you chose to walk away. You may feel lonely during this time. You may feel your lowest. You may feel there's no more left for you, that love isn't for you. Honestly, the problem is you're too forgiving. You're too giving. Stop letting them take until you have no more to give. Love isn't the fantasy you placed upon it. Love isn't fighting for someone to love you back. People always think of heart break and assume there's no other direction, picking up the pieces should've freeing. Picking up the pieces should be liberating. Walking away from someone who placed pain and misery in your life should be a blessing. Please, don't let someone make you feel losing them is the end, it's a blessing in disguise. You lost every hope, but they lost every chance at love with you, that's everything.

You are enough,
you will always be,
in case you were wondering.

Remember, you are enough.

I know it's hard to believe, when you feel you're the reason for every ending to every love story you thought would make it. I know you put in a lot of time, love, and energy to every soul who came close to being the one. I know you lost more times than you won. I know you feel as if you're broken, because every time you open yourself up to someone new, they end up hurting you too. It's time to open your eyes, stop letting those walk in your life with a free trial to your heart. You don't know who they are, what their intentions are, or their character. You only know what they show you, give them time to reveal their true colors before you give them every part of you. Stop trusting souls with your heart so easily. You want to be loved, so you give them a chance, but you end up emptier than you were before.

Don't sacrifice your worth for a chance to be loved.

Don't be afraid to let them know your worth. Set the standard high, if they can't match your energy, or inspire a greater you, let them know when they don't deserve you.

Don't lessen your worth to be accepted.

Don't lessen your worth to be loved.

To be respected, set your standards high, truly live by them. The more you allow yourself to be defined by everyone, the more lost you become. You're the writer to your own life, you make the rules. Your heart is a sacred place.

Only keep genuine souls in. If you find your
energy's not being matched, the inspiration
being lacked, let them know it's time to part
ways. You don't need to keep anyone who
brings more misery than peace. You don't need
to be uncomfortable for the sake of someone's
comfort. You don't need to be afraid to tell
them they don't deserve you, even if you're not
quite yet sure of your worth, letting them go is
a start. *You're on the right path*.

When you're no longer blindsided and you set the boundaries and foundation, there's a less chance of getting hurt if you're accepting what you deserve.

We all fell victim to love.

We all were a sucker for love.

We all did it for love.

We all have neglected ourselves at one moment because of love.

We all were meant to believe love was pain.

We all didn't know our worth.

We all didn't know to set boundaries, a foundation, so we accepted what we thought we deserved.

We all were once blindsided by love; we didn't realize we weren't accepting a healthy love.

Once you know, don't fall victim to love, again.

My heart's big, but not big enough to be a convenience. **My love doesn't deserve to be taken for less than it's worth**.

<u>I love in the form of all, or not at all</u>.

I overstayed my welcome before knowing our story was expired, I overplayed it. I rarely led with my mind, it's either my heart or intuition. I pay close attention to the dishonest love. I remember the times I was used, overlooked, and forgotten. I never forgot the love I tainted chasing the wrong ones. I never forgot the love I let pass me because I was broken. I let my heart become a weapon against me, I let my heart become my weakness. I may have once settled for convenience, but now I'm aware of the heart I have isn't a burden. **My love doesn't deserve to be taken for less than it's worth**.

<u>Stop letting yourself go unappreciated</u>,
you deserve so much more
than to be someone's second best.

Broken: For the Ones Picking Up the Pieces

I feel intensely, when I love, I love unconditionally. I don't love any different, I can't. When I love someone, their troubles become mine too. Their trauma are my demons too. I try and heal them, I become invested in everything they have going on; it becomes my problem too. I take too much on from everyone I love, I don't know when to separate myself from the love. I always thought loving someone meant going above and beyond, but that line stops once I neglect myself for their need. I didn't realize I was hurting myself, trying to be a savior to their heart. I didn't realize I couldn't be a hero to someone who couldn't be saved. I didn't realize it wasn't my mission to mend them back together. I didn't realize their heartache wasn't mine to recover. I didn't realize I lost myself just to be someone they couldn't be without. I didn't realize I stopped loving me. I had to let go once I realized they were only bringing me down, not bettering themselves. I couldn't keep that energy surrounding me. I made a vow to only do what's best for me, what brings me peace.

I'm not sorry I had to set you free.

When it's time to move on, don't think of how hard it is because you'll always get discouraged. *Remind yourself of the scars*. *Remind yourself of the pain*. **Remind yourself of the strength taken from you**. It's time to accept the things you can't change and reclaim your power.

Moving on is hard because you think of how hard it's going to be to leave it all behind you. What exactly are you leaving behind that makes you sad? The good times? In this case, those good times didn't outweigh the bad. Remember the scars. *Remember the pain you endured while fighting for them to feel your love.* Remember everything, not only the good. Open your eyes and see the real in the one you loved, when you do, you'll see the love they didn't have for you. You'll see the love that only lived within you. You'll see the dishonest intentions. You'll see the strength you left behind. Your power isn't gone, you just forgot your worth for a moment, it's okay, **you will make it**.

Stop going back to the same person who damaged your outlook on love, who made you change your ways and turn cold, there's nothing left for you to give or receive, it's time to leave history where it belongs.

We have a habit of going back to where we
once found comfort. We have a habit of
latching ourselves completely, to souls who are
hard to love because we have so much to
prove. We have so much love to give, we just
want them to know our love is worth it. We
don't understand we're wasting time trying to
prove to them, what we're desperately trying to
prove to ourselves, that our love is enough. We
have a habit of going back because we feel it
was us that couldn't get it right, so we try again.
We don't realize we just weren't meant to align.
We don't realize we just weren't meant to
provide love to someone who couldn't feel us,
because we were too intense. We keep trying,
because when we love, we love all in or it's not
worth it. We keep trying until we get it right,
until we realize, it never will, and we need to
set ourselves free from the fight.

When's a time you fought for a love that
wasn't worth the fight?

_____

_____

_____

_____

_____

_____

_____

_____

_____

_____

_____

_____

_____

What have you changed since then?

_____

_____

_____

_____

_____

_____

_____

_____

_____

_____

_____

_____

_____

_____

_____

1. Don't overlook the signs
2. Don't use your love as an excuse to keep fighting for someone who doesn't love you back.
3. Don't be afraid to walk away
4. Don't let yourself come close to losing yourself to protect a love that has failed you.
5. Don't use love as a weapon, you will be the only one picking up the pieces.
6. Don't prove your love to those who don't care how deep your love goes.
7. Don't change who you are, or how your heart beats to be accepted, or loved.

If you feel the need to do any of these,

it's not love.

Instead of saying "it will hurt more when I let go" speak into the universe, "It will feel better" healthy and positive energy always! **You're better off without anyone who doesn't appreciate you.**

<u>Don't ever blame yourself for how you love.</u>

The level of intensity isn't to be sorry for, never apologize for having a huge heart. Be proud of the heart you were gifted, protect it. Stop letting people tell you different just because they're afraid to feel it.

The way you love may not be for everyone.

To be truthful, it won't be for everyone. Some souls are still searching for who they are. Some are busy dwelling in the past or fighting for the one who hurt them. Some are so cold from the last, they won't even feel your warmth. Don't ever apologize for the intensity of how you love, it's a gift not many know how to embrace. Having a huge heart is a blessing in this cold world, treat it like so, and handle it with care. Your heart is a blessing, never a burden. Please remember that before you give your heart away so easily.

"Repeat: **I am good enough. I am love.**
My love is not too much. I am worthy of
everything great in the world."
Until you believe it because it's true. So
many of us forget our worth trying to help
someone find theirs.

Write from positive affirmations for
yourself on this page.

Having a big heart could burden you if you're so open to helping everyone when it could burn you. It's okay to say no if it doesn't bring positive light to you. It's okay to say no, in general. You don't need to be at the need of everyone you love, sometimes our loved ones aren't the best influences and it's not up for you to save them.

You can't save anyone; you just love them hoping your positive influence reaches them. Don't ever think it's wrong to be selfish. *It's okay to choose yourself in any situation*, especially when it may hurt you.

Love is something truly special when it's real. Some may take advantage of your love. Some may see how far your love will go. Some love you, but not as much as you love them. Some are damaged and may damage you. Don't over give your heart. Don't spread yourself out thin, to the point you have no more to give. Don't keep trying to save someone who can't be. Don't neglect yourself by always being at the need of everyone. Say no if they love you, they will understand, they should know how important you are. They should know you need to love yourself too, they won't be selfish, they won't want to lose your love, it's special, *it's sacred*, I hope you understand that too, **protect it**.

Having a big heart is beautiful, but don't overextend yourself trying to prove to anyone your love. **It's okay to be selfish**. It's okay to protect your heart. It's okay to say no. If someone loves you, they wouldn't risk losing that love, they wouldn't make you choose.

My love has always been real, my intentions have always been pure. My love has overwhelmed some. I've been asked to "tone down" my emotions. I've been asked to hide my feelings. Basically, I've been asked to be a completely different soul. My love was never for the weak. My heart has always been big and too much for some people to understand. I never understood why my heart did the opposite and made others run, but I know now they weren't ready for my love. At one point in my life I utterly convinced myself I was too much, that my overly emotional self-drowned people with my love. It took some time to see that lovingly intensely was not a problem, that it was only unhealthy when it wasn't reciprocated. My love never hurt anyone, it was only when I was convinced it was too much, or never enough, **their toxic ways blinded me from remembering my own heartbeat**.

You're afraid to open your heart to another soul, to let them inside your world knowing they can hurt you at any moment but trusting them not to. It's scary to fall for someone without knowing the outcome. *Love may seem terrifying*, but **it's the bravest act a human can behold**.

A heart so big and a soul so gentle,

you should never be convinced

you're hard to love.

The error we all make,

is trying to be loved

without loving ourselves first.

The error we all make, is trying to be loved without having knowledge of love for ourselves. We give all we have to the one we love, or the one we're pursuing, and we forget to give to ourselves. We forget we need to set the foundation of how we wish to be loved. We forget love isn't love if we can't love ourselves. We forget no one can appreciate everything we are if we don't know our worth. You will settle for love in the lowest form of what you fantasized it to be, when you're unsure of your own worth. Your insecurities cause you to settle for anyone who shows interest, because their presence makes you forget the loneliness you feel. They help you see yourself in a different reflection, which can be misleading. If you can't know your worth, anyone can tell you who you are, and you'd believe them. Before you love someone, or allow them to love you, please, **love you first**.

Have you found your worth?

Have you loved you, first?

_____

_____

_____

_____

_____

_____

_____

_____

_____

_____

_____

_____

_____

_____

This heart was never a home to you, but I
tried and tried to make it one.

I should have known better, than to force my love upon you, when you didn't deserve it. My intentions were always pure, and real. My love for you was honest. I should have never made myself open to you when your love never felt like home to me. I was fighting for you to feel me, I didn't realize the definition of love I fought for was the longing of love I needed to fulfill within me first.

Don't ever think that loving too much is a form of weakness. Don't change your love language because of a wrong one, keep giving your authentic self until someone loves all of you.

If you question your heart, please, trust your intuition. It never lies. It never makes you feel uncomfortable for no reason, so open your eyes. Don't keep letting souls in who will hurt you more than they'll ever love you. Don't keep letting everyone walk all over you and expect you to deal with their toxicity. You're allowed to walk away when things are no longer healthy. It's okay to not have an explanation on choosing yourself, they don't need closure after damaging you all the times you didn't have the vision. It's okay to choose what makes you happy in the moment, what makes you feel alive, in that moment. The universe doesn't make you question the love, intentions, and character of someone for no reason. There's more for you, when it presents to you, don't overlook it. Don't try to hide what you're faced with it. Accept not everyone will be a permanent soul in your story, some are only here to remind you, **you deserve better.**

Treat yourself like the beautiful soul you
are and stop taking care of everyone while
neglecting you. It's healthy to love
someone so much, just don't abandon your
own needs to make them happy.

What you're currently going through isn't the end. The bad days represent the strength you have. The bad days remind you of the good you have surrounding you. The bad days should never make you wish to never feel again. No one emotion will only be felt. It's normal to feel differently, both happy and sad. It's a good balance. Don't be afraid to take a break when you need to reset. Don't overthink saying no to plans just because you don't feel like going. Don't over worry about situations you have no control over. I know sometimes it's hard to adjust not always being the savior, but it's time to take care of yourself. It's time to reflect on all the good you've done for everyone and realize you can only love them; you can't make anyone change, it's up for them to. Focus on bettering yourself. Focus on the better days. **Healing the soul is just as important as healing the heart**. Don 't let one bad day turn into the rest of your life, it's up to you to change that.

Sometimes you need to hurt a bit

to understand the blessing in it.

I pray for everyone who still believes being

heartless will get them far in life.

I pray you understand, abandoning your

heart will never bring you to peace.

If you need to tell someone how to love
you, that's a sign right there it's not pure.
Someone who loves you won't ever need
directions to your heart.

Let me start by saying, this isn't telling someone they way you wish to be loved, using love languages. There's nothing wrong with expressing your love languages. What I'm trying to say, if you need to tell someone how to love you after they had their chance, or many, there's no way of getting it right. You shouldn't need to put them on the path to your heart. Some people feel if things come back together after being broken, it's a sign it's meant to be, that's not always true. Sometimes when things become tainted, it's a sign to keep it moving forward and not look back. Pure love will always work, you won't ever need to question it.

What are your love languages?

1.

2.

3.

4.

5.

6.

7.

Narcissists will truly suck the life out of you,

don't stay.

Souls are placed into our lives in the
moment we need them. They find their
way to us—to love us, to teach us, and
sometimes leave us. It's unhealthy to
blame your heart because you chose to
believe everyone is meant to stay.

I let souls back in too many times, the word sorry lost meaning. I gave directions to my heart after being hurt too many times. I didn't realize I kept telling people how to love me, wasn't going to make them love me. *I was creating my own heartache.*

I let people in too easily.

I let myself open to souls too quickly.

I let my heart go into the hands of ones who

showed me attention when I was searching

for love, I couldn't see the difference. I

thought I could create love, instead I only

created pain.

I was never dumb; I always saw the real when it was presented to me. I was only blind when it came to love, when *I was so desperately trying to be loved*.

Love me while you have the chance, or
don't love me at all. Once I'm gone, I'm
gone, *you'll be forced to love me from afar*.

I've set you free. How you feel about me doesn't have anything to do with me, it's a reflection of your own insecurities.

Our time expired.

Our connection will always be cherished.

I will always love you, but I don't need to

keep you in my life to do so.

They know they lost you when they try and use your success as a weapon against you, and make it look as if you're selfish for wanting what's best for you. Never let anyone make you feel the need to dim your light for them to feel comfortable. **They don't deserve to love you**.

Some people only love you

at their convenience,

stop giving them open access to your heart.

If you love someone, but they aren't reciprocating that love, let them go. If they come back, there's a chance the universe is testing you, to see if you still haven't learned the lesson they dealt you. **It's your choice**, keep repeating the same story, or grow.

Everything in my life came together, once I stopped trying to force what wasn't meant to be in the picture.

I believe the universe creates chaos to
show me what's no longer healthy. I
believe the universe brings them back
down my path to test me. I've discovered
my peace, there's no way I'll ever go back
to what took that from me.

I decided to start new, something about picking up the pieces and putting myself back together didn't feel right. The only way to grow, was to let go the version of myself that endured so much pain.

Apologize for your wrongs, *take accountability for your behavior*. Don't expect things to fade away, that's where pain comes in.

The thing about being broken, *you never stay broken*. You can always pick up the pieces and mend yourself back together.

Broken: For the Ones Picking Up the Pieces

Now tell me, were you ever broken, or were you just blind, lost, and unknown of the worth you behold? We are never broken if we're still breathing. We are never broken if we're able to keep loving. It's just, sometimes we focus on making others happy, loving others, and helping them find themselves we forget to take care of ourselves, too. We feel broken because the love we thought would last, failed us, but not only that, we overstayed the welcome and created more pain. We fight for love and many times don't understand what love is, because the love we fought for was only felt by us, it was more in the terms of lust. We feel broken because we're lost after searching for love in ones who can't give it to us. We hide, become unavailable to newcomers because we're afraid that maybe they'll love us how we always prayed, but we keep investing in the wrong ones to give them a chance. I never understood the chase, the constant choosing of the wrong souls to match with, but sometimes they give you a moment of fulness, of comfort, completeness. I understand now the constant rush is short lived. Some live with an agenda, to not genuinely love you the way you deserve, because they're currently searching for who they are too. It's important to remember we're all imperfect, but we all are perfect in our own ways. It's important to remember, we're all made to love, just sometimes we confuse the definition of love just to feel it. A least, we hope we get the chance to. So please, you were never broken, stop letting yourself believe you are, because of a couple bad ones. Build yourself first, I promise there's happiness there.

I thank you always, from my whole heart, for always supporting and taking a chance on my work. I hope you are satisfied always with the content I provide. I give you the rawest form of love, and everything in between, nothing but moments in time from my many experiences.

I pray you all know, there's always a time in our lives we will feel our lowest, but if you're still breathing, there's always room to keep living. Don't stop believing. Don't stop giving your all. Don't stop fighting for what you believe is right. Don't be afraid to do what's right for you. I'm praying for you, always.

Instagram: @Moonsoulchild

Twitter: @Moonssoulchild

Facebook: @Moonsoulchild

For more books:

Moonsoulchild.com

Or Search on Amazon: Moonsoulchild